W9-AKV-970

DATE			

The Library of PIRATES™

The Barbarossa Brothers

Sixteenth-Century Pirates of the Barbary Coast

Aileen Weintraub

The Rosen Publishing Group's
PowerKids Press™
New York

To my DaddyMonster, who was the most fearless of them all

Published in 2002 by The Rosen Publishing Group, Inc.
29 East 21st Street, New York, NY 10010

First Edition

Project Editors: Jennifer Landau, Jason Moring, Jennifer Quasha
Book Design: Michael Caroleo and Michael de Guzman
Layout: Colin Dizengoff

Photo Credits: p. 4 by Mica Angela Fulgium; pp. 7, 11 © The Art Archive/Dagli Orti; pp. 8, 20 © Mary Evans Picture Library; pp. 10, 19 © AKG London/Erich Lessing; p. 12 © CORBIS/Bettmann; p. 15 © The Art Archive/Musée Condé Chantilly/Dagli Orti; p. 16, 20(background) © The Art Archive/University Library Geneva/Dagli Orti.

Weintraub, Aileen, 1973–
    The Barbarossa brothers : sixteenth-century pirates of the Barbary Coast / Aileen Weintraub.
        p. cm. — (The Library of pirates)
Includes bibliographical references and index.
    ISBN 0-8239-5799-3
    1. Barbarossa, d. 1546—Juvenile literature. 2. Admirals—Turkey—Biography—Juvenile literature.
    3. Pirates—Turkey—Biography—Juvenile literature. 4. Arouj, d. 1518—Juvenile literature. 5. Pirates—Africa, North—Biography—Juvenile literature. 6. Pirates—Mediterranean Region—History—16th century—Juvenile literature. [1. Barbarossa, d. 1546. 2. Pirates.] I. Title.
    DR509.B22 W45 2002
    961'.023'092   2001000619

Manufactured in the United States of America

Contents

The Red-Bearded Brothers

The Barbarossa brothers were two of the most feared **corsairs** of the 1500s. Corsairs were pirates who sailed the Mediterranean Sea, taking land for their governments. Corsairs **plundered** ships and towns for riches. They also captured people and sold them as slaves. Arouj and Kheir-ed-din were **Muslims** who were loyal to the Turkish government. The brothers set up their **headquarters** on the island of Jerba, between the port cities of Tunis and Tripoli on the North African coast. From this spot it would be easy to attack enemy **Christian** ships. Soon the brothers became known for their red beards. They were given the name Barbarossa, which means "red beard" in Italian.

◄ *Arouj and Kheir-ed-din Barbarossa were Turkish corsairs who boarded enemy ships to capture slaves and steal goods.*

Arouj's Battles

Arouj was the first of the two Barbarossa brothers to become successful. By 1504, Arouj was sailing along the North African coast, which was also known as the Barbary Coast. He stopped at the port city of Tunis and made a deal with the king there. The king let him use the harbor. He also agreed to protect Arouj from enemies. In return, Arouj gave the king a share of everything he captured. Arouj **defeated** many local **chieftains** and freed many ports from Spanish Christian rule. He captured many ships, riches, and slaves. He is most famous for taking over Algiers in North Africa. Arouj died during a land battle in 1518. It is said that he fought until his last breath.

BARBARIAE ET BILEDVLGERID, NOVA DESCRIPTIO.

This map in Latin showing the North African coast is from an atlas, or book of maps, made in 1570.

Kheir-ed-din sent riches to the sultan of the Ottoman Empire so the sultan would let Kheir-ed-din work for him.

A Strong Empire

After Arouj's death, his brother, Kheir-ed-din, became a great naval **commander**. He was an educated man who spoke six languages. Kheir-ed-din wanted to work for **Sultan** Selim of the Ottoman **Empire**. This empire was a powerful Muslim force in the Mediterranean. The capital city of this empire was Istanbul in Turkey. Kheir-ed-din sent many riches to the sultan. In 1533, the new sultan, Sultan Suleiman, agreed to see Kheir-ed-din. Sultan Suleiman wanted to make sure that the Christian navy stayed away from his land. He was hoping that Kheir-ed-din would help protect his empire.

Kheir-ed-din Meets the Sultan

Sultan Suleiman

Kheir-ed-din took his time traveling to meet Sultan Suleiman of the Ottoman Empire. When he finally arrived in Turkey, he had 40 **vessels** filled with gifts for the sultan. These gifts included lions, gold, jewels, and slaves. The sultan needed Kheir-ed-din's help organizing a navy before the Christians became a **threat**. The sultan appointed Kheir-ed-din Kapudan Pasha, meaning **admiral in chief**. Kheir-ed-din left the sultan during the summer of 1534. He sailed westward to **ravage** the coasts and ports of Italy. The plan was to take as much land away from the Christians as possible. That way the sultan would have more power.

This map in Latin from a 1570 atlas shows Britain, Italy, France, Germany, Russia, and the Barbary Coast. ▶

The galley shown here was rowed by slaves who
were beaten if they didn't row fast enough.

A Corsair's Ship

A corsair's ship was called a **galley**. Each ship had about 90 galley slaves to row it. Although we know today that slavery is **cruel** and unjust, it was very common in the 1500s. Muslims captured Christians and used them as slaves. Christians also used Muslims as slaves. The slaves were forced to sit on wooden benches. Their feet were chained to the benches. There were four men for each oar. They had to row for hours at a time without stopping. They were given very little food. Galleys were heavily armed with cannons, guns, and spears. A corsair would attack an enemy ship by pulling up alongside it and climbing aboard. Once aboard, the corsair and his men would steal all the riches and capture the people as slaves.

Capturing Land

Kheir-ed-din promised Sultan Suleiman that he would capture the city of Tunis, which was on the North African coast. This land was under Spanish rule. In 1534, Kheir-ed-din planned his attack. When the ruler of the city heard about Kheir-ed-din, he ran from the city in fear. Kheir-ed-din captured Tunis after the ruler left. This was important for the Ottoman Empire. Tunis was in a good location and would provide safety for Muslim corsairs raiding Christian ships. Emperor Charles V of Spain heard that Kheir-ed-din had taken over Tunis. He sent a spy to Tunis to organize a **revolt** against the Muslims. He hoped that the spy would either **bribe** or kill Kheir-ed-din. The plan failed. Kheir-ed-din found out about the spy and put him to death.

Emperor Charles V ruled Spain from 1519 to 1556.

A Tough Fight

Emperor Charles V of Spain did not give up his plan to get back the city of Tunis. In 1535, he sent a large **fleet** commanded by Admiral Andrea Doria. As soon as Doria entered Tunis, he captured part of Kheir-ed-din's fleet. Kheir-ed-din was prepared for the attack. He had his best-armed galleys waiting in Bone, a port city between Tunis and Algiers. He was waiting for Emperor Charles V's land army.

Kheir-ed-din tried to stop the army but failed. Within Tunis, thousands of Christian slaves broke loose. They found a supply of weapons and attacked the Muslims. The Christian navy entered the city and took over. Charles V had control of Tunis once again.

◀ *This engraving by an artist named Hogenberg shows the Spanish fleet capturing Tunis in 1535.*

Kheir-ed-din's Surprise Attack

Kheir-ed-din left Tunis when he realized that he had lost to the Christian forces. Emperor Charles V of Spain thought that Kheir-ed-din would gather more men and attack Tunis again. Instead, Kheir-ed-din decided to attack a place the king did not expect. This place was the Balearic Islands in the Mediterranean. Spain owned these islands. Kheir-ed-din tricked the people on the islands by flying Spanish and Italian flags on his ship. The Christians thought that their own fleet was coming home. Kheir-ed-din easily took over the town, capturing thousands of Christian slaves. Then he carried all of the treasure back to Algiers on the North African coast. Emperor Charles V was shocked.

After the Battle of Tunis, shown here, Kheir-ed-din planned an attack against the Balearic Islands in the Mediterranean.

Kheir-ed-din was a big threat to Christians and their land.
They wanted to get rid of this fierce corsair once and for all.

More Battles

In 1538, Christian leaders decided to combine their forces to get rid of Kheir-ed-din for good. Admiral Andrea Doria led the Christian troops once again. The troops waited near the Greek island of Corfu. Kheir-ed-din and his large fleet were in a port near the Greek mainland. This port was sheltered mostly by land. There was no way Doria could get his fleet into this port. Doria would have to make Kheir-ed-din sail out to sea. Doria sailed into the open sea and Kheir-ed-din went after him. Doria couldn't get his fleet back together fast enough. Kheir-ed-din attacked Doria's ships one by one. He did not lose any of his ships or men to Doria's fleet during the chase. This was a major defeat for the Christians.

The Chief of the Sea

In 1543, Sultan Suleiman of the Ottoman Empire sent Kheir-ed-din to take over the coast of Italy. At one point, Kheir-ed-din captured a governor's 18-year-old wife. He agreed to release the girl's parents from slavery if he was allowed to marry the girl.

Kheir-ed-din soon reached the French Riviera in France. He set up headquarters at the port of Toulon. He continued taking over cities until 1544. This was when Francis I, king of France, bribed the Muslim forces. The king gave them gifts so they would go back to Istanbul. Kheir-ed-din died of a fever in his palace two years later. When he died, people all over Istanbul cried out, "The Chief of the Sea is dead."

Glossary

admiral in chief (AD-muh-rul IN CHEEF) The head of the navy.

bribe (BRYB) Money or a favor given in return for something else.

chieftains (CHEEF-tenz) Leaders of tribes or other groups.

Christian (KRIS-chun) A person who follows the teachings of Jesus Christ and the Bible.

commander (kuh-MAN-dur) A ship's officer just below the captain.

corsairs (KOR-sars) A type of pirate who sailed the Barbary Coast.

cruel (KROOL) Very mean.

defeated (dih-FEET-ed) To have won against someone during a contest or battle.

empire (EM-pyr) A group of countries, lands, or people under one government or ruler.

fleet (FLEET) Many ships under the command of one person.

galley (GA-lee) A long, narrow ship or boat that moves by use of oars, used mostly for war or trading in the Mediterranean.

headquarters (HED-kwar-turz) A center of operations where leaders work and give orders.

Muslims (MUZ-limz) People who believe in the Islamic religion.

plundered (PLUN-durd) To have robbed by force.

ravage (RA-vij) To destroy something by using violence.

revolt (rih-VOLT) To fight or rebel.

sultan (SUHL-tan) The ruler of a Muslim country.

threat (THREHT) A person or thing that might cause danger.

vessels (VE-sulz) Ships or large boats.

Index

Web Sites

To learn more about the Barbarossa brothers, check out this Web site:
http://school.discovery.com/homeworkhelp/worldbook/
atozhistory/b/046100.html